Elke Erb
Das Gedicht ist, was es tut
A poem is what it does

Herausgegeben von
Matthias Kniep und
Thomas Wohlfahrt

Edited by
Matthias Kniep and
Thomas Wohlfahrt

Elke Erb

Das Gedicht ist, was es tut
A poem is what it does

Deutsch – Englisch

Übersetzt aus dem Deutschen
ins Englische von Shane Anderson

**BERLINER REDE
ZUR POESIE 2018**

Wallstein Verlag

Bibliografische Information der Deutschen Nationalbibliothek
Die Deutsche Nationalbibliothek verzeichnet diese Publikation
in der Deutschen Nationalbibliografie; detaillierte bibliografische
Daten sind im Internet über http://dnb.d-nb.de abrufbar.

© Wallstein Verlag, Göttingen 2020
www.wallstein-verlag.de
Vom Verlag gesetzt aus der Stempel Garamond
Umschlaggestaltung: Marion Wiebel, Wallstein Verlag, Göttingen
Druck und Verarbeitung: Hubert & Co, Göttingen

978-3-8353-3856-2

Inhalt

Das Gedicht ist, was es tut 7

A poem is what it does 47

Kurzbiographien 87

26.1.2018

Das Gedicht ist, was es tut

Wie fange ich an?
Ich habe da zwei kleine Gebilde aus Worten mit der
                                 Überschrift »Poesie«.
Das eine ist vom April 2017. Das andere aus dem vorigen
                                 Jahrhundert, vom 4.7.1979.
Es heißt sogar »Poesie pur« –

Poesie

Ich sagte plötzlich beim Frühstück mit den beiden hier auf
                                 dem Land:

Man ist ja irgendwie immer elf, und Geli: stimmt, sie sei
                                 immer zwölf.

Ei!

Poesie pur

Ein Esel und ein Hahn,
die Freundschaft geschlossen hatten,
gingen einst miteinander spazieren in einem Park.

1970

Die Dichter wohnen in den Jahrhunderten,
Dieser in jenem, jener in diesem, einer lappt über
Der andere mittendrin wie der andere, der auch mittendrin wohnt.

Schön und gut. Endler erstreckt sich von 50 bis 90 in seinem.
Sonst wohnen auch die Dichter in Wohnungen wie dieser,
Die z. B. der Endler besitzt, Quartierchen fünfter Stock,
Badlos, Hinterhaus, Außenklo, aber mit Sonne.
Wenn der Dichter Endler seinen Kopf zum Fenster raus-
streckt,
sieht er nach, ob die Müllkübel leer sind.

Adolf Endler, Gedichte, Essays und andere Prosa, geb. 1930, gest. 2009, also viel später, als im Gedicht steht. Wir waren 10 Jahre verheiratet, von 1968 bis 1978. Das Gedicht habe ich vorgetragen bei einer oppositionellen Veranstaltung gegen den Schriftstellerverband der DDR. Die der Partei, der SED, sie nannte sich das »Hirn der Klasse« (nämlich der Arbeiterklasse) gehorsamen Genossen im Verband sollten und wollten uns beherrschen.

20. 9. 1970 / 17. 2. 2017

Die Olympiade

Jammerschade, daß es nicht gelingt, diesen Traum zu erzählen, der so merkwürdig seltsam skurril kurios absonderlich war. Wir saßen in den Zuschauer-Rängen, Vorbeimarsch der Begräbnis-Prozession. Vier Junge Pioniere, zwei aus den unteren, zwei aus den oberen Klassen, die einen schwarzen Kranz und Schleifen tragen, sie weichen, sich mit steifer Ehrerbietung verneigend, ein wenig beiseite (hier herüber, jenseits liegt das grüne Länderspiel-Oval): eine Dame unter schwarzen Schleiern, Gattung Stuten*fisch*, russisch: ryba, Vollbart landgüteriensis spectabilis namens Maier, russisch M*ajor* überholt die Pioniere, reiht sich zwanzig Meter vor ihnen ein auf dem nackten Weg.

Die Dame, seine Tochter nämlich, hatte sich verspätet, holt auf, kommt die Treppe herauf, wehklagend, wirft ihre Arme im Schleiertuch, ruft verzweifelt: »Und seine Bibliotheken, ach, und seine Bibliotheken immer wieder verloren, nun, die zwölfte, die schönste von allen, sein Ein und Alles – da stirbt er.« Ich folge ihr, heirate sie.

Bin der Verwalter seiner zwölf Bibliotheken, in einer parkettierten Beletage. Erledige jetzt gleich seine reinen zierlichen Korrespondenzen, Sachen auf dem höckerbraunen Rokoko-Schreibtisch. stelle mich stante pede neben die geschwungenen, auf das Parkett gesetzten Beine des Sekretärs, rufe, mir über die Einzelheiten noch nicht im Bilde, meine Frau herbei, um von ihr zu erkunden die anderthalb Räume der weiteren Beletage. Mit dem Mann aber, unserem Toten, fahre ich spazieren, ich, die Nebenbei-Frau, echte, Kollegin, Kameradin – »ich und du« – Ringe hab ich an den schlanken Fingern wie Blumen im Grase.

Das Auto hielt an hinter Schilf bei mehreren Kiosken, hintereinander gebaut. Jene nach rechts sind geschlossen. »Warte mal«, sagt der Geschäftsmann, geht nach links, »irgendwas wird sich schon finden, das eine können wir sicher. Können wir bestimmt«.

Baden? Hinter dem Schilf entdecke ich, in der Vormorgenstunde ganz allein, eine Truppe von schlanken japanischen Turnern in orangenen oder türkisenen Trikos. Sie gehn hin und her auf der Bade-Matte und erörtern etwas erregt, dabei schlagen sie sich in die Hände, mit dem Rücken der linken Hand in die Fläche der rechten, und gehn hin und her auf der Matte. Bis ins 20. Jahrhundert waren sie eine Streitmacht der DDR, höre ich.

Später erzählt man, Jugendliche hätten sich mit minderjährigen Äffinnen eingelassen. Ich will es nicht glauben.
Man fährt mich zu den medizinischen Häuschen; eine Äffin hält unter ihr Kinn eine runde Metallplatte gepreßt, die Schwester klickt den Verschluß auf, das Kinn blutet, andere Wunden habe ich auch gezeigt bekommen, doch sind sie mir nicht mehr erinnerlich.

24. 9. 1970

Es ist manches auch ungereimt

Wir Neffen schätzen die unverwelkliche Pflanze, das
                                      Immergrün
nicht das unsterbliche, immer, Pflänzchen, die Immortelle,

doch den streng beschnittenen immerdar grünenden
                                      Lebensbaum.

Nicht ergreift die Seelen der Toten die Immortelle, die
                                      Strohblume.
Ich möchte mein Buch übersetzen in das unsterbliche
                                      Immergrün

und will nicht gehn auf dem Friedhof besehn
den untoten Lebensbaum.

Die bunten Strohblumen meinen, sie seien schlau,
ungleich den anderen Blumen, die leben und sterben dumm.

Kaum ist die Zeit um,
fallen sie auch um.

Die Staubfänger halten sich länger, Jahre, da schau.

Ein verirrtes Insekt, vor Kälte erstarrt,
trägt ihren Samen, was sonst, das Leben ist hart

7.12.1975

Reim dich, oder ich freß dich

Der Zug ist in den Bahnhof eingefahren.
Das leergetrunkene Glas steht auf dem Tisch

Den Schutzgöttern gedankt, den römischen Laren!
(Ihr Name, der gesuchte, ist gefunden.)

Den Alten hat man rehabilitiert.
Die Schuldigen jedoch nicht inhaftiert.

Die wurmstichigen Balken sind ersetzt.
Die Nimmermüden können ausruhn jetzt.

Die Wunde ist bestrichen und verbunden.
Was haben wir zum Mittagessen? Fisch.

1.3.1977

Widerstand

Mir traten neulich moralische Aspekte des Wortspiels vor Augen, es wird ihm ja Selbstgenügsamkeit, Aussonderung, Beliebigkeit, »Amoralität« vorgeworfen.
Sind die Worte Diener, ist der Autor der Herr (oder der volkstümliche Witz?!). Vorsicht! Ein Herrentum pfuscht

in diese Sicht. Und wie stellt sich der Herr zur Realität? Da nimmt man demnach irgendein Wort, trennt es von seiner Familie und seinen anderen sozialen Beziehungen ... – Der Spieler dagegen läßt ihm sein Leben.

Zufall ist ein Plus in einem System. Als zufällig setzt das herrschende System verlogen das unterdrückte herab. – Das Wortspiel aber befreit das unterdrückte System. Es heitert es auf. Liebe deinen Nächsten, spricht die Bibel. Nicht von klassenbedingter Unmenschlichkeit.

Kann man dem Spieler nicht vielleicht vorwerfen, daß er die Worte über sich herrschen läßt – An seiner Statt? – Das wäre verschleierte Herrschaft.
Oder tanzt er dem Hörer und Leser auf der Nase herum, weil er sich nicht einordnen kann, überhaupt asozial ist? Haupt und Nase sind verwandt wie Bruder und Schwester. Da spricht man nicht von sozial. Laß dir, lieber Spieler, die Freiheit nicht nehmen. Wer unter uns wird bestreiten, daß du doch womöglich einer guten Sache dienst? Du bist der Produzent (spätmarxistisch nunmehr gesehen), und die Worte sind die Produktionsmittel, du bist der Mensch, und die Worte sind die zu beherrschende Natur, das ist gewiß wahr. Weitergedacht könnte man ja auch sagen, das Wortspiel sei ein Gegenbeispiel gegen die Umweltverschmutzung, dieses Resultat der Zivilisation, ein freies Spiel abseits von freier Marktwirtschaft und Monopol.

Einzuwenden wäre gegen das Wortspiel, sein menschliches Gutsein und Gewährenlassen, daß es doch nötig sei, Widerstand zu leisten. Aber ist nicht im Leben auch Güte real?

1978

Abwechslung

Gleich hinter der Grenze im Hammer-und-Sichel-Emblem:
Die rote Sichel – den roten Hammer im Munde –
                                              ihre Spitze
so dicht nahe am Griff, als wolle sie Fahrkarten knipsen.

Vor einer großen, dunklen, aber auch blühenden Kastanie
ein zweites, aber ihre Sichel, rot wie die erste, nur geöffnet
und ihre – diesmal längere – Spitze erhebt sie,

als sei sie ein Vogel nun in der Welt und bitte um Futter.

Bert Papenfuß gewidmet zum 60.
Er ist ein bekannter Dichter, geboren 1956. Er gehörte in
der DDR zur Prenzlauer-Generation, seit langem ist er auch
selbst Veranstalter, Stichwort Rumbalotte.

6. 10. 1979

Ich gehe auf einen Weg, er glänzt,
aber ich habe zu wenig mitgenommen.
(Er glänzt von leichten Füßen, die strahlen)

Ich kehre zurück mit jener Reue,
in der man wieder alles liebhaben will,
lieber behalten hätte. Um es

noch mehr zu verlieren,
was erstrebt und im Dunkeln ist,
aber vor der jeweils größeren Liebe, die es zulassen wird,

so augenweitend sich erhellt,
daß es die mir jetzt eigenen Formen,

(bis zu tiefer Schwärze wie verfault
der beklommenen Sicht)

(aber hell und warm immer im Licht
der neuesten Windungen)

in den letzten Schatten der Erübrigung und Erlösung stellt.

Der Trieb, mich zu sichern, läßt mich sogar
auf optische Täuschung deuten: bei Licht sieht man, dort
war nichts.

Auch möchte ich ja fliehen und fühle mich in der Falle,
höre ich jemanden sagen: Ich erinnere mich, daß du ...

Ich verenge die Augen vor dem, was ich hören werde.
Und gehe heimlich, verhülle Gegenwart, Namen, Beruf.

Spüre aber das Flimmern und erkenne klar
die schwärzesten Schrecken, atmen
die Liebe.

Frühjahr 1988

Das nächste Gedicht ist ein Text über das Schreiben, denke ich.

Bewußtsein –
erst produziert es das Tote,
dann das Lebende.

Eine todfressende Pflanze,
so, wie ihr Leben wächst.

Der Tod, den sie frißt,
muß ebenso wachsen:
bis an die volle Größe sich

aus*wachsen.*

20.6.1994

Das folgende Gedicht habe ich geschrieben während eines Poesiefestivals in der Hafenstadt Rotterdam.

Das Gefühl des Gewinns
bei der Überlegung, Gedichte seien Erkenntnisträger:

nämlich; hast-du-nicht-gesehen schwimmt schulterhoch
und umgeben teichgleich ein allgemeines Interesse
so, als habe es im Sinn, zu erkunden, was ist,
und existiere gewiß.

Von dieser falschen Höhe fällt dann der Blick
hinunter auf etwas in Ellbogenhöhe: Geschäftstips.

– Nun darüber Wellengrün, Wasser klatscht an den Quai.

18.11.1995

Wenn ich von der Form ausginge,
dann gleichfalls als von einer existentiellen. Also eine
                      Gleichstellung der Strukturen.

Auch während des Schreibens das Suchen.
Und während des Lesens fremder Texte das Suchen.

Dieses zweite blickt auf die Interessen des Kunstwerks: wie gelingt es.
Und: was bringt es?

Das erste, was es bringt, ist das Gelingen (oder Mißlingen).
Das Gelingen setzt voraus die Bedingungen.

Dahinter noch geht mit beim Schreiben wie beim Lesen ein poetologisch innovatives Interesse.
Als sei 1.) die Sprache das Leben (was sie ja auch ist);
     2.) das Gedicht-Individuum ist ein selbständiges
                      Subjekt.
Zugleich sind beide »im Dienst«.

Wenn ich das »so oder so« dort finde, lese, sehe ich, es kann besser angehn als »so oder so«. Es kommt das und das heraus.

Das sind sehr allgemeine Aspekte, die wohl jeder kennt: Jenseits-Sichten.

19.8.1998

Rohstoff, jungfräulich

– ein allgemeingültiges, nicht nur den eigenen Part
belichtendes, und / oder ein an die als Kultur geführte
                                        Tradition

anschließendes, mithin auch einschließendes
(das jeweils Eigene)

Denken keineswegs, niemals:
Der sich stets versorgende Blick hat keine Zeit zu –
hungern (lungern?). Und ungern.

Das bringt mich (um nun etwas zum Kinn Untriges
ins Spiel zu nehmen) – bringt mich dahin (angenommen,
ich fragte), die optische Anordnung

unwillkürlich zu haben, aus der Tiefe
per Pause unbenutzter (während er schläft) Kommißstiefel
Äußerungen zu erwarten: wurzelechte oder: kernholzige ...

9.3.2000

Schade, daß die jeweilige Unmöglichkeit sich nicht verbindet mit ihrer jeweiligen Überwindung. Das verhält sich so bewußtlos zueinander. Bewußtlos, als steckten Stückchen Totes überall dazwischen. Die sind uns über.

Heute morgen bin ich zwar angeregt, aber traurig. Farbe: grün. Die Stückchen Totes: weiß oder *noch* ärger. Füchtet-euch-nicht-Farbe.

Ganz so, wie mir auch unmöglich ist, mir vorzustellen, jemand in Paris tritt an den Tisch, zieht den Stuhl hervor und setzt sich. – Nein, weg!

Zwischen hier und dort und Übersee geht die Welt unter.

7.4.2000

Ästhetischer Schub: Gerade dachte ich, wie das Ästhetische denn eine Existenz gehabt haben könne so imposant, von solcher Präge-Leitkraft, daß man die poetische Rede, diese Formen wußte und wahrte, das Formen-Reich, das diese Formen miteinander wohl ausmachen. Ein neuer Ton, eine neue Schwingung, die an den Korpus kommt (etwas Stehendes wie Stehendes Heer, das eine Funktion zwar hat, aber – außer in Bewegung – nicht funktioniert).

7.4.2000 am selben Tag

Formierte sich das Tonangebende ständig?
Es ist fraglich, wie das Ohr heute mißt. Fügt sich ein neuer Ton zu einem als ewiger Vorrat aufgefaßten Vergangenen? Man darf nichts nehmen außer mit Recht, außer erneuernd, außer mit Sinn …
Eine Anspannung ist da, aber sie hört wohl mehr auf dem großen Ohr als auf das tradierte Klavier.

12.4.2000

Poesie ist lebensnotwendig. Sie leistet gesellschaftliche Arbeit, und sie kann sie auf keine andere Weise tun als poetisch.

12.4.2000 am selben Tag

– ein neues Thema: Das Verhältnis der anderen Künste zur Poesie. Da geht sie durch *mich* als Medium durch und wirkt mit meinen Mitteln ihr Werk weiter.
So, wie ich es auch selbst tue: Ohne zu fragen, etwas zum Medium machen um seinetwillen.
Das ist wohl nicht so bei der außerhalb der Literatur existierenden Poesie? Oder doch? Aber doch: Sie muß ja nicht erst geschrieben werden!

13.4.2000

Wieso reagiere ich anders, wenn ich auf literarisches Mißlingen bei mir stoße, auf etwelche unangebrachten Griffe, Wendungen, anders als sonstige Diensttuenden vielleicht? Ihr Raum grenzt sie ein, meiner ist frei. Er verlangt es. Unbedingt, wie man sagt, ein freies Müssen.

Da wird ein allgemeines Terrain sozial verlassen. Erkennbarkeit wird verlangt. Und gegeben. Befreiend. Auch wenn sie wegen sozialer Einschränkung von den anderen nicht genommen werden kann. Es sei denn etwa in befreiendem Zorn.
Den Apostel Paulus befreite eine Vision, so wurde er der Apostel. Der Märtyrertod war die Folge. Paulus hatte die Liebe gepredigt, als freie Gnade Gottes und Bewährung des Glaubens.
Zorn.
Die einen müßte man Opfer nennen, die anderen nicht, obwohl sie ja gleich beschränkt sind sozial.
Die Frage wird leidenschaftlich und hart, wenn sie nach dem Verrat fragt.
Verrat ist, zu behaupten, etwas anderes sei nicht möglich.
Eben das ist es, was unsereins aufregt, uns aufrecht erhält.

29.6.2000

Poet, dein Publikum, das dich erwartet, sitzt vor allem in deiner eigenen Seele!

6.7.2000

Das Ich, das sich auflehnt, den Tod nicht versteht, ist wohl das gleiche, das, als es irgendwo das Wort »Nebenzimmer« hört, (»dann eben im Nebenzimmer«); gereizt reagiert, wie auf eine Zumutung, nachdem es ein paar Tage zuvor den Anblick der Flußbreite mit den Hafen-Speichern am anderen Ufer eine Weile, nicht ohne sich zu nähren an ihm, geduldet hatte.

11.7.2000

Die geringfügigen Wendungen ins Freie, jene Veränderungen an jemandem, am Text von jemandem, man kann sie bemerken, auch wenn man ihn vorher nicht kannte und die Anzeichen als jeweils konkrete Fortschritte auch nicht erkennt; sie übermitteln sich aus Ursache eines Generalisierungseffekts des – im jeweils Individuellen – allgemeinen Käfigs.

15.11.2000

Ich gehe von gelebten existentiellen Situationen aus, alle im Tagebuch zielen auf sie, holen Sichten auf sie und sie entwickeln sich während des Notierens von ihnen her.
So entscheiden sie.

Ein poetologisches Betreiben ohne sie kenne ich nicht.
– Es interessiert mich nicht zuerst, wie ein Gedicht zu bauen wäre. So daß ich ein Material für es suchte. Ich gehe nicht zu gegebenen Formen. Umgekehrt: Ich schreibe etwas, und dann sehe ich, oh, das ist ja ein Sonett. Einmal auch eine Art Sonett geschrieben, einmal ein Haiku.

Das Haiku:

Das Gedicht erscheint.
Sobald es erschienen ist
ist es verschwunden.

9.12.2000 / 18.9.2016

Dreizeiler

Es dunkelt schon in der Heide.
Man fängt irgendwie an und endet bei sich.

Besser als umgekehrt.

10.3.2001

Ein Grundsatz ist sicher: ein Vers ist ein Vers. Wenn man sie leblos deklamiert, dann rutschen sie in eins zusammen wie Zusammengeschraubtes beim Fahrrad. Die ungeteilte Verbindung ist dem Unfesten gleich, unartikuliert.

am 23.9.2001

fällt mir auf, daß ich nie zum Tagebuch greife, um ein Gedicht zu schreiben.
Zwischen den Anregungen – das ist ja übrigens ein hübsches Wort hier, – zwischen den Anregungen dieser und aller anderen Art gibt es vorweg keinen Unterschied im Beweggrund. Auch ein gutes Wort.
Erst beim Eintragen deutet sich da eine poetische Struktur an. Öfter steht dann am Ende »Gedichtverdacht«. Und es ist oft auch viel später eine zu erkennen. So habe ich in den letzten Büchern Datierungen von früheren Jahren nacheinander, im letzten Buch, »Sonnenklar«, gehen sie sogar bis ins vorige Jahrhundert zurück.

5.12.2001

Unterschiede

Seit dem Herbst fiel mir bei meinen Tagebuch-Einträgen, wenn sie Gedichte wurden, eine fehlende Einhelligkeit auf. Sie bildeten Räume, die einen, die anderen nicht.
Eine fast ortlos präzise Dichte nach innen bei »Rohstoff, jungfräulich« in dem Buch »Sachverstand« (erschienen im Jahr 2000).

Ich nehme an, das ist ein Text-*Typ*.

Der Rohstoff-Typ ist leidenschaftlich, holt heraus, spitzt zu, der andere Typ verlangt dienende Disziplin. Präzision. Nichts blitzt da auf.

16. 10. 2004

Es setzt auf mich

Das ist ein Werkstück, wartet.
Werkstück in mir wartet.

Beinahe täglich kommt wer
oder was, lenkt ab.

In mir heischt es, zürnt es.
Spürt. Wirkt. Werkstückt.

Keine Lockung. Kaum guten Muts. Ich
bin die Fee für es. Kommt die Fee zu ihm,
hofft es, lebt es auf. Sie gibt ihm dies und das
aus ihrem Gang. Aus welchem Gang?
Dem allgemeinen.

Von dem dort, in dem allgemeinen,
dem allgemeinen Gang der Dinge, Angetroffenen
und Abgefallenen, von dem Ablauf, der es übergeht,
bekommt es dies & das. So wäre es ja gut.

Aus dem, was sich so zuträgt.
Zufällig. Das Werkstück lebt dann auf.
Es ist ein Werkstück zwischen Tod und Leben.
Wie zwischen Berg und Tal.

Es ist nicht sicher, daß es eine Chance hat.

Offengelassen haben, ob es eine Chance hat,
wird zu seinen Vorzügen gehören,
wenn es eine Chance hat.

Sowohl im Ganzen als auch in den Einzelzügen.

Wartend und offenlassend.
Seins ist ein Präsens-Partizip-Prinzip. Verlaufsform.

Sonst wird es nichts.
So wird es vielleicht gut.
So ist es eine Fee, die kommt wie eine Gnade.

Die aber nicht verlockt kommt. Nur wie hinbeordert.
                                                    Ungewiß.
Unsicher kommt. Sich hintrollt. Trottet deppdumm
hin zu ihm, dem wartenden.

Es stochert. Heischt.
Es setzt in abträgliche Spannung.

Abtragen tut gut.
Daß ich mich zu ihm wende, tut mir gut.
Obwohl es guttut, lockt es nicht.

Seine Substanzen, Angelegenheiten
existieren ohne mich. Sonst wären sie nicht seine, eigene!
Das muß so sein.

»Ohne mich« ist ein Motiv der Hinsicht:
Es trennt, es unterscheidet.

So entsteht Indifferenz, ich nenne sie.
Indifferenz entbindet dich und mich.

Sich versäumen
und versäumen und versäumen.

Fremdgehn. Nebenher.
Einem Thema nachgehn, das nicht seins, des Werkstücks, ist.
Doch. Im Hintergrund. Im Versäumen.

Dieselbe Formel gilt, sie herrscht, auch sonst:
Ich weiß, daß ich nicht tue, was mir guttut.

Ein Prozeß aus nichts als mir, in dem
nicht ich entscheide, scheinbar.

Hoffnungslosigkeiten tagen:
frühere, viele, auch erloschene, Perspektiven.

Tagen wie das Tageslicht,
so ungerufen und unführbar.

14. 2. 2007

»Ich bleibe nichts schuldig« – wohllautet es – nachdem ich vermutend sah, sehend vermutete: ich erfasse die Zeit im selben Gedicht (und Herzkranzgefäß), das auch das biologische Ausleben aufnimmt und das geistige Reifen bewirkt, dieses Es-lösen, Sich-Lösen ...

Das Wort »vermuten« kennt die Art der Sicht: ein Spüren, es sucht nichts, es findet, genannt wird die Zeit, sie ist, kurz gesagt: ein Geschehen. Und zwar positiver Art dank der Paarung des Biologischen mit dem Geistigen. Ich habe Hunger – ich esse. Man könnte eine solche Folge auch Lösung nennen. Und umgekehrt ein geistiges Reifen auch Wachsen. So ist es freilich mehr als ein bloßes Erledigen. Dem Wort Gedicht wird hier das Körpersein zugedacht. Und umgekehrt dem Geistigen das Vollenden. Wie es sich im Gedicht auslebt, gibt dem Gedicht die gelöste Individualität.

9.12.2007

Klärung

Jetzt ist die Seele unerreichbar,

während ihr falscher Widerschein
ganz das Gegenteil vermeint zu melden.

Er ist falsch, vermeint jedoch.

Schau hin, sage ich mir,
in das Schwarz, das bodenlose
absolute Jenseits.

Das Schwarz dort siehst du als Schicksal, Irrsal
der unselbständigen, habunseligen
Seelen-Inhaberin –

Es könnte alles allenthalben hiesig sein,
rechtens sein,

hiesig rechtens hintergangen sein,
schau nämlich hin, schau zu,

schau hinterher – enttäuscht –
dem jähen Rückfluß jeder je
Begeisterung.

N., wie er betrunken war so oft,
und aufdringlich
im Saal

an dem und jenem
weißen Tisch.

Kahl. Und dahinter ist – wie Klarheit / Klärung –
dann nichts als nichts,

nichts weiter als ein abgefallener Blutdruck
in deinen Zellen allenthalben

unter den gewohnten Skalenstrich
wie tot.

4. 1. 2008

Schwung

Es schottet sich ab verwahrt sich
will bloß dasein, scheint es.

– ? Nein. Ist gefesselt.
– Ergrautes gefieder schläft abwärts.

Engelsflügel erhebt, erlebt man nicht.
Schwingen wie engel.

Nur die harfenellenwelle, wogend,
harfenspiel-ellbogenwelle.

Als indem der kater niemals ist der vogel,
niemals: nonsens, niemandem ein vogel,

aber eine elle in der länge
elle ohne hand, gerecht zu sein,

welle doch am ehesten im sprung
des tigers – tigerwelle,

– und mit weniger (der kater)
vorzüglich auskommt

auch gewöhnlich nicht gejagt wird,
grauer kater achtbarer, gemessener ehre –

grauer kater und orangener, gefleckter, schwarzer –

Hattst du etwa vorzubringen vor,
daß auch teufel teufel auch beschwingt sind –
anfangs?

14. 1. 2008

Es tut sich auf: Mißlingen Panorama Landschaft wie wir es eben nur in einem Blick erfassen. Eine Vielgestalt, sehn wir eine Landschaft oder etwas ähnlich Statisches ... Aber es wird ja erlebt in einer komplexen Dynamik, deren Bewegung im Lesen und im Erleben die Komplexität »aufschlüsselt«.

Infolgedessen gibt es gar keine Rettung als schnelles Erfassen. Rasch, nicht anzuhalten, zugleich komplex, nicht simplifizieren.

(Die Aussicht eröffnet ein Scheitern)

Was zeigt sich:
Der Rand sammelt alle Ideen,
die Mitte ist trüb und sauer.

Das ist insgesamt: als seien Sie dabeigewesen und noch dabei und künftig dabei.

Gestern war ich draußen mit (zu leiser) Musik, Klavier
– Schumann Viele kleine Stückchen. Es unterhielt.
Der Arbeitseinsatz am Text verfällt rasch, sobald ein Intensitätsplus auftaucht –

Was sagt man dazu –
Die Überlegungen hier eröffnen ein Gedicht, das die Situation mit seiner poetologischen Bravour erfaßt, bezeugt, erweitert.

15.1.2008

Der Reiz, etwas zu folgern aus den Zutaten, der Reiz, etwas zu schreiben, die Spur von dem, zu dem. was ich schreiben will, schreiben sollte,

führt scharf nach draußen, ja jagt mich, läßt mich scharf hinausjagen, ihr Objekt-Subjekt, Subjekt-Objekt das ich bin.

24.8.2009

– faktisch könnte man sagen, was von außen überrannt worden war, ist wieder zur Stelle und schaut, yes.

11.2.2012

Milliardäre

Milli
Zahlen, Bodenschätze
ar
fruchtbare Erde
däre

11.2.2012

Weltniveau

Unvorstellbare Armut
und Verbrechen aus Armut

die Kutsche wählt
das Gespann mit dem Kutscher

16.6.2012, 6 Uhr 47

Nein

Ich will nicht die, die ich kenne, will ich nicht.
Eine andere will ich. Eine anders Gequirlte.

Will nicht in den Tag der vorigen gehn.
Nicht stumpfe Fortsetzung.

Das äugende Licht
äugt vom Balkon,

Fliesen, Wandputz-Zerfall, Stuhlgestäng.

»Keine Verbindung.«

Aber doch, Großmutter,
fange ich gleich die Übungen an.

Wecke die Muskelstränge.
Fuchs, sag, wie sonst.

11.1.2013

Spricht eine Schwäche Meinung

Ich sage / sie sagt /
hin & wieder: ich will nicht
wie aus einer Grundschwäche
spricht eine Meinung Schwäche
spricht eine Schwäche Meinung

tue mir nicht genug
Unentwegt steigen Verhältnisse auf …

Finde mich flüchtig gegenüber
Begründe sie nicht

Gegenüber ehemals Baum
ehemals Gebirge
See
erscheinen, verharren

Ich nicht

Halte die Waage nicht
Halte, begründe
nicht

20.6.2014

Das leuchtet ein

Der kluge Blick (auf etwas hinunter – textwärts)
und der gütige – sie sind zum Verwechseln ähnlich.
Leuchtet ein!

14.10.2014

Gedichtherkunft: Tagebuch.

Herzweh, einsames

Da ist guter Rat teuer.

Niemand ist da.

Dieses Nichts ist unausbleiblich.

18.10.2014

Den ganzen Tag über war mir kalt. So ein einfacher Satz. Und ich galt ewig als unverständlich. Naja, ist nicht meine Schuld. Ich wette, so ein Satz ist nirgends zu finden schriftlich. – Hm, ähnliche wohl doch. Nein, ich meine ja *schriftlich*.

16.12.2014

Das Ausland: Georgien.
Das Datum meiner Reise dorthin läßt sich nicht genau ermitteln.
Die erste Reise war mit Adolf Endler und Rainer Kirsch 1969, dann fuhr ich mehrmals allein.

Erinnerung Ausland

Von oben kam,
von lehmgelber Höhe,
eine Reiterin (Zigeunerin?)

buntgekleidet lässig
seitwärts sitzend
herunter

unten auf dem lehmgelben
Weg stand ich vor einer Reihe
von drei bis fünf Walnußbäumen,
größeren, beständigen,

wenn ich nachdenke,
unbedingt drei bis fünf,

nicht etwa nur
drei oder vier, hätten dann
bis fünf nicht gereicht,

an denen die Reiterin
nachher vorbeikäme, ehe
sie denn zur anderen Seite
hinaufritte wieder, Ausland.

15.1.2015

Bei all dem in Teilen Bewegten, sich weiter Teilenden und Vereinenden – Sichten und Festgekeilten Fixierten auch

Man weint vor Mandelstams Wolfshundsjahrhundert als dem Ich einer Göttin ungeteilt heftig Eruption Erschüttert neu und unendlich

Davor war ja Freude gewesen, als ich ging draußen Musik im Ohr und Schritt

7.2.2015

Hübsch naiv:

2300 – Merke gerade
– komplett schwarze Nacht umher –

daß es auch gefallen kann,
den Tag abgenudelt zu haben,

wenn man sich angestrengt hat.
Na – nur zu!

April 2015

Das Aus hat (wie
der Laut sagt)

keinen Garten.

7.7.2015

Ich lese im Bad: Nathalie Sarraute – »Sagen die Dummköpfe«

»Es gibt nichts Rührenderes
auf der Welt«*

rerrerrerres
Das Wort rührt selbst.

* *Nathalie Sarraute, eine französische Schriftstellerin russischer Herkunft (geboren 1900, gestorben in Paris 1999,*

»*Sagen die Dummköpfe*« ist, schreibt Wikipedia, ein Roman von ihr, Deutsch von Elmar Tophoven).

August 2015

Maxime

Struktur-Verständnis: ich muß alles, was mir von/an Menschen begegnet als Ausstattung mit einem Gerippe auffassen, wie das Tier als Ganzes vor- und durchprogrammiert ist; wir ja eher vor-, aber das festsitzend, unbeweglich genug eine lebendige Frische, Kraft, wird auch festgehalten von einer Unkenntnis über sie usw.

9.8.2015

Wache auf, schwitzend (zur Uhr – 1:21). Warum nur läßt das Gemüt die anonyme Last nicht los oder diese es? Sie ist ja auch ichig. Nettes Wort. Jede gute Laune, ist erst verdient, scheint es, scheint *mir*: Woher kommt sie, Erinnerung an *etwas*. Nie *mich*. Oder Ablauf. Jetzt war eben noch wieder der Wille, Antrieb, dieses übliche Muß (wir sind Partner), die Einnahmen aufzuschreiben, einer der Fleiße der Zivilisation, Ich-Teil. Nämlich wohin im PC. Kann ich wen fragen? Die Welt wërolt Menschwelt wër Mann, Mensch scheint es zu kennen.

Hier in der Niederschrift komme ich zu mehreren kleinen Überraschungen bereits, noch nicht aber zu dem Gefühl mit ihnen. Sie helfen auf die Welle guter Laune – Fischsprung, das ist gute Laune anonym? fast. Mit der Niederschrift gekommenes Entkommen. Das schwarze kleine Fenster – Nacht neben mir. Und weiß darin die Trotzkibücher aufgeschlagen, bin ja jetzt im Bett ohne meine Brille.

Gehe ins Bad, lese weiter, immer weiter im Trotzki, langsam begreifend, aber nun geht es stetig. Monate so. Gut. Begreifen entwirft Gänge, Durchsichten. Lese weiter ein Stück mit dem Bleistift zum Anstreichen dabei, wie gestern, als es nicht mehr ging in der Hitze. Jetzt schon 29 Grad. Der gute große Echt-Sommer, der Seins macht, wir sind ja nur Eigenschaften von ihm.
Tja, trotz der argen traumatischen – in der Traumkammer – Rechnungsträgerei, der ja öfter quälenden. Das ist die Last, die, selbst wenn man sie abschiebt – »ist ja nicht nötig, mußt du ja nicht unbedingt jetzt« – ihren Platz behauptet dumpf.
Während hier oben: drehe mich um, blicke ihn entlang, den erstaunlich langen braunen Dachbalken zur anderen Seite hin. – Messe ihn: 3,17 Meter lang, mein Blick dachte: ein Baum so hoch!

6:12. Wieder aufgewacht, nicht fröhlich, nach etwa 3 Stunden Schlaf, ach, da ist ja auch der niedrige Blutdruck – hatte ihn vergessen. Ruhe noch etwas.

Nicht so gewaltsam.
8:30. Geschlafen. Aber dasselbe: 27 Grad, bei bedecktem Himmel.

17.9.2015

Ich will nicht zuviel sagen. Ich habe einen
Brunnen im Kopf. Im Hof. Brombeeren.
Ahso.

10.3.2016 / 28.7.2017

Rahmenlos

Dörflicher Chorgesang
Tragödie = Bocksgesang – trages: Bock,
singt und tanzt mit Bocksmasken: Chor.

Aus dem Seßhaften, sieh!, hinaus.
Tier-Energie.

Sonst ja keiner als *dieser*
Schwung. Im Fest.

Sing, sing, was geschah ...
Keiner ward je gesehen ja.
Zogen einst fünf wilde Schwäne ...

Es weiß die Heerschar sich mit dem Führer eins.

Oh, ich lege im Hirn eine Klappe um.
Um Artus das war noch kein Führerkult.
Seine Ritter stiegen vom niedersten Rang
in die edelste Adelskultur.

Wolltest du Macht haben je? Nicht wahr, nie?

Wer
wollte Macht. Der
Kretin Hitler, der unterentwickelte
Unmensch Stalin.

Und welch ein verjährter Stolz
zwang Vornehme zum Duell?

– Eben *weil* ein Thema aus dem Zusammenhang tritt, folge ich ihm. In das, was sich ihm auftut. Es lebt ja dann.

19.3.2016

Wir unterhielten uns so (am Telefon), ich weiß nicht, wie ich darauf kam, das Stichwort war »Alex«.

Ich war da beim Physiotherapeuten, und weil die Masseuse die Muskeln gelockert hatte, taumelte ich noch leicht. Als ich auf den Alexanderplatz vortrat, hielten mich zwei Polizisten wohl deshalb an und verlangten den Personalausweis. Während sie in den Ausweis schauten, fragte ich, über sie hinblickend: »Wen suchen Sie denn hier auf dem großen leeren Platz?«

Nämlich, während vordem auf dem Alex in den Gesträuchrabatten noch Hasen hoppelten, hatte man stolz zu sein auf zwei Hochhäuser nun.

Und Helga erzählte, vor ihrem Haus stand ein Stasiauto, und als sie herauskam, sagte sie: »Ich gehe jetzt zum Verband der Bildenden Künstler, dann in die Kaufhalle, und in so anderthalb Stunden bin ich wieder da.«

Heute ist der 19.3.2016. Ich dachte, ich dokumentiere das mal.

Ein Jahr später hörte ich am Telefon von Helga noch eine andere Erinnerung, für mich war sie ein Gedicht, es lautete so:

Die Nachrichten

Ich – unter dem Tisch – bin 6.

Wenn der Krieg vorbei ist,
darf man beim Essen reden.

Helga Paris, meine Freundin seit langem, so alt wie ich, eine Fotografin, Mitglied der Berliner Akademie.

26.3.2016, 5:38

Nichts weiter:

In der Leere fürchte ich mich.
Fürchte ich mich davor, mich zu fürchten.

Die Tauben gurren, unten ist Erde,
Boden. Schwarze Nacht. Oh, nein,

habe das Rollo hochgezogen,
es ist schon hell. –

3.10.2016

Eine Reaktion auf Ernst Bloch: Freiheit und Ordnung, Abriß der Sozialutopien, Reclam Leipzig 1985

Das Wort Klassenschranken – bezeichnet eine die Ausbeuterklasse beschränkende Hemmung – die Arbeiterklasse ist keine Klasse, sondern die Folge der Ausbeuterklasse.
Die Menschen haben ständig Hierarchien gebaut seit der »Urgesellschaft«.

Die Ratio: Es sollte etwas richtig sein von Rechtswegen …
Hier blickt der Verstand. Sein Sinn ist: Bestehen statt Untergang.
Hat aber vor sich: Tatütata. Naturrecht ist die Erfindung des Verstandes als Regime. 17. Jahrhundert.

Die Ratio kann blind sein, der Verstand nicht.

Der Bürokrat will blind sein, sonst fliegt er ja,

für Jan Kuhlbrodt, meinen Leipziger Freund, er schreibt Gedichte, Romane und Essays

14.12.2016

Gedichtverdacht

Liege auf dem Bett, bäuchlings, lese

(erhole mich) (an geistiger Disziplin).

Das Kreuz tut etwas weh.

Als ich darauf aufmerksam werde,

wölbt sich vor mir ein Brückenbogen hoch auf.

Warum, denke ich, der jetzt?

– Meinem Kreuz gebe ich Luft …

Unten haben wir Grasufer … Wasser …

Gedichtverdacht.

29. 5. 2017

Tagebuchbeute aus dem Bertelsmann-Taschenlexikon:

Petschenegen,

Stammesverband turksprachiger Völker
Stamm Baumstamm abstammen
stämmig

untermischt mit sarmatischen u. finnisch-ugrischen Gruppen

flogen da wie Samenwolken aus der Luft her

»ugrische Gruppen« *finnisch & ugrisch verquickt*
wann wo wie

Semikolon

seit Ende des 9. Jh.
– nachdem sie aus diesem herauswaren also

... nördl. des Kasp. Meers, steht da,
dieses verzipfelten Hellblaustrumpfs,
auf Erden, größten Binnensees

im Kampf mit den Chasaren, steht da,
von denen *nach W* (Westen) *gedrängt,* wo

sie sich in Süd- (*Stabreim*)
rußland nieder

ließen, **B**eutezüge führten (*weiterer Stabreim auf* **b**)
nach **B**yzanz, Ungarn, Rußland
(*Rußland ist riesig*) **b**is

Jaroslawl der Weise die **P.**
1036 besiegte.

Dem Stabreim oben verlorenes **s**. Von
nachdrängenden Kumanen nach
Ungarn u. Bulgarien abge-
drängt

(*viel, aber genug nun geulkt*)

gingen die **P.** in der dortigen
Bevölkerung

auf.

Petschenegen.

Der Zischlaut machts.

Ich erkenne dies als Gedicht.

8.6.2017, 4 Uhr

Seit etwa zwei Stunden wach. Will schlafen. Schalte das Licht aus. Blicke nach rechts durch das kleine Fenster. Dahinten hinter dem Laub duckt sich ein Rot.

Lese ein Heft über Derrida, Einleitung S. 13: Er habe sich in der ersten Phase (1962–72, geb. 1930) vorwiegend mit der Erscheinung, bzw. den Spuren von »Wahrheit« »beschäftigt«, während in den späteren 70er Jahren »die ästhetischen Modelle und Experimente einen Schwerpunkt bilden«. Ein gesteigerter Anspruch also, was die Dichte betrifft.

– Von dort aus zur »Ethik der Diskussion«, zu einem neuen theoretischen Ansatz.
Satz:
»Liege wach neben dem Morgenrot.« – – –
Licht aus. Vor dem Fenster schaukeln die weißen
                                          Holunderblüten.
Licht an: Schreibe es auf. Vielleicht wird ein Text daraus. Wenn ich es vielleicht erreiche, diese fernöstliche Feinheit (Japan, China) herzuzaubern.
(Nicht ausgeschlossen.)

24.7.2017

Natürlich bin ich unsicher beim Warten auf den Flixbus, nicht ich fahre ihn, bin Objekt. Bei anderen, Normalen, ist das kein Problem, das Objekt gewinnt eine Selbständigkeit. Bei mir, dem Schreib-Subjekt, dirigiert ein objektives inneres Subjekt. Sie sind so etwas wie Partner. Das innere scheint blind und taub. Das äußere wird von den Resultaten oft überrascht.

5.8.2017

Eine seltsame Bemerkung im August: Ich erkenne beim Abschreiben der Tagebücher, daß ich die Sprache eigenständig aktiviere (über das hinaus, was ich gemeinhin lese), und zwar auf eine natürliche, unangestrengte Art. Ob das ein Entwicklungsprozeß ist? Da es ein einfacher Prozeß ist, bestünde Hoffnung für jeden, daß er es auch könnte. So daß die allgemeine Sprache sich mobilisierte. Die üblichen Anstrengungen der Lyrik- und Wissenschafts-Sprache verfehlen den Prozeß.

16.8.2017

Im Sommer auf dem Lande

Von Zeit zu Zeit, grad da
lauf ich aus dem Haus

um um das Haus herum
zu laufen auch

eine Zeit

Damit höre ich auf. Ende.

31.12.2017

Mir fällt ein, rückt ins Gemüt, bei meinen Lesungen muß ich den Leuten guttun, sie sollen es merken. – Wenn ich das will, gelingt es mir auch.

– Zuguterletzt aber ein anderer Schluß.

Das Gedicht ist, was es tut.

Ich lese noch ein Gedicht aus dem Buch »Sonanz«, von dem man sagen könnte, das Gedicht ist, was in ihm geschieht. Wohl auch ein Tun, doch ein freieres, von dem die späteren gewiß profitiert haben. Seine Schreibzeit: 2002 bis 2006.

8. 7. 2005

Warnung

Die Welt ist voller Angelhaken. Volkslied und im Chor.
Die Welt ist voller Volksgesänge. Das Tal ist leerer
                                          Hirschgeweihe.
Ich träume Knarren Karren. Sonniger Morgen, träume
                                          Karren knarren.

Hinterm Hause das Gefild ein nackter Brustkorb.
Auf und nieder atmend. Rippen.

1/26/2018

A poem is what it does

How do I begin?
I have two small formations of words here with the title
»poetry.«
The one is from April 2017. The other is from the previous
century, from 7/4/1979.
It's even called »pure poetry« –

Poetry

I suddenly said during breakfast with the other two here
in the countryside:

Somehow you always stay eleven, and Geli: true, she's
always been twelve.

Well!

Pure Poetry

Long ago, a donkey and a rooster,
who struck up a friendship,
went for a walk in the park.

1970

The poets live in the centuries,
This one in that one and that one in this one, one overlaps
The other in the thick of it, like the other one who also
lives in the thick of it.

Well and good. Endler goes from 50 to 90 in his.
Apart from that, the poets live in apartments like this one,
Which, for instance, Endler owns, small rooms on the
                                          fifth floor,
No bathroom, in the rear building, communal toilet,
                                          but with sunshine.
When the poet Endler sticks his head out the window
He looks to see if the garbage cans are empty.

Adolf Endler, poems, essays and other prose, born in 1930, died in 2009 – i. e. much later than what's in the poem. We were married for 10 years, from 1968 to 1978. I recited this poem at an event opposing the GDR's writers association. Those comrades obedient to the party, the SED (The Socialist Unity Party of Germany), called themselves the »brain of the class« (namely, the working class) and were supposed to dominate us and they wanted to dominate us.

9/20/1970 / 2/17 2017

The Olympics

A crying shame to be unable to relate this dream that was so extraordinary strange bizarre curious peculiar. We were sitting in the spectator stands, a funeral procession marching by. Four *Junge Pioniere* (Young Pioneers), two from the lower classes and two from the upper, were wearing black wreaths and ribbons and bowing with deep reverence, they moved a little to one side (to this side, on the other is the green oval for international matches): a lady under a black veil, genus mare*fish*, Russian: ryba, full bearded manoriensis spectabilis by the name of Maier, Russian Ma*jor*, passes the Pioneers, gets in rank twenty meters directly in front of them.

The lady, namely his daughter, is running late, catches up, runs up the stairs, wailing, throws her arms into the shroud, and desperately calls: »And his libraries, oh, kept losing his libraries and now, the twelfth one, the most beautiful of all, his one and all – that's when he dies.« I follow her, marry her.

I'm the caretaker of his twelve libraries, housed on a *piano nobile* with parquet flooring. I'm about to settle his immaculately delicate correspondences, matters on a knob-cone-brown rococo desk. I'm standing posthaste right next to the curved legs of the secretaire that's on the parquet and summon, without yet knowing the details, my wife so as to learn about the other one and a half rooms of the rest of the *piano nobile* from her. But with the man, our dead man, I go for a ride, me, the woman on the side, the real, colleague, comrade – »me and you« – I have rings on my slender fingers like flowers in the grass.

The car stops behind some reeds at several kiosks, built one next to the other. Those to the right are closed. »Wait a second,« the salesman says, goes to the left, »something will turn up, we can be sure of that one. We can be, for sure«.

Go for a swim? All alone in the small hours, I discover behind the reeds a troupe of slender Japanese gymnasts in orange or turquoise jerseys. They're going back and forth on the bath mat and are heatedly debating something, at the same time they are clapping their hands with the back of the left hand in the palm of the right and they're going back and forth on the mat. They were a military force of the GDR into the twentieth century, I hear.

Later, someone says the youth have become involved with underage female apes. I don't want to believe it.
Someone drives me to the little medical house; an ape is holding a round metal plate pressed under her chin, the nurse snaps the cap, the chin is bleeding and I'm shown other wounds but I can't remember them anymore.

9/24/1970

Some things lack rhyme

We nephews treasure the fadeless plants, the evergreen
not the always, immortal, little plant, the immortelle,

but the severely trimmed forever greening arbor vitae.

Not the souls of the dead, the immortelle grasps, the
                                          everlasting daisy.
I want to translate my book into the immortal evergreen

and don't want to go to the graveyard to look
at the undead arbor vitae.

The radiant everlasting daisies think they are smart,
unlike the other flowers that live and die ignorant.

No sooner is the time over,
they too fall over.

The dust collectors last longer, years, look there.

A lost insect, frozen with cold,
carries their seeds, what else, life is hard

12/7/1975

Rhyme or I'll eat you

The train has arrived at the station.
The downed glass is on the table

Thanks to the Guardian Deities, the Roman Lares!
(Their name, the one searched for, has been found.)

The old man has been rehabilitated.
The guilty, however, have not been incarcerated.

The worm-eaten beams have been replaced.
The tireless can now take a break.

The wound is coated and bandaged.
What are we having for lunch? Fish.

3/1/1977

Resistance

I was recently reminded of the moral aspects of puns, they are often accused of being solipsistic, withdrawn, arbitrary, »amoral.«
Are the words servants, is the author the master (or a folkloric joke?!) Careful! A mastership blunders into this perspective. And what position does the master take to reality? According to this, you take any old word, separate it from its family and its other social relations … – the player in contrast lets it live.

Chance is a plus in a system. As chance, the ruling system dishonestly demeans the suppressed. – The pun, however, frees the suppressed system. It lifts it up. Love your neighbor, the Bible says. Not out of class-determined inhumanity.

Can one accuse the player of letting the words prevail over him? – in his place? – That would be concealed control.
Or is he dancing on the nose of the listener and reader since he cannot be classified, and is antisocial in general? Head and nose are related like brother and sister. One doesn't speak about what's social there. Don't give yourself, dear player, the freedom. Who among us would dispute that you may have served a good cause? You are the producer (now seen from a late-Marxist perspective), and the words are the means of production, you are the human and the words are of a dominating nature, that is certainly true. Taken further, you could also say that puns are a counterexample counter to environmental pollution, this consequence of civilization, a free play away from the free market economy and monopoly.

An objection to the pun, its human wellbeing and tacit approval, would be that it is in fact necessary to offer resistance. But isn't benevolence in life also real?

1978

Relief

Right behind the border inside the hammer and sickle
                                            emblem:
The red sickle – the red hammer in its mouth – its tip
so close to the grip as if it wanted to clip a ticket.

From a large, dark, but also blooming chestnut,
a second one, but its sickle, red like the first one, is open
And its – this time longer – tip lifts it,

as if it were now a bird in the world and asking for food.

Dedicated to Bert Papenfuß on his 60th birthday.
He is a well-known poet, born in 1956. He belongs to the
»Prenzlauer Generation« in the GDR and he has been an
organizer for a long time, keyword Rumbalotte.

10/6/1979

I'm walking on a path, it is sparkling
but I haven't brought enough with me.
(It's sparkling from light feet that beam)

I turn back with that kind of remorse
when you want to hold everything dear again,
would have preferred to keep it. In order

to lose even more
what is pursued and in the dark
but before the greater love that will accept it,
it becomes so plainly obvious
that it places the forms that are now my own

(as deep a blackness or rottenness
of the apprehensive point of view)

(but bright and warm always in the light
of the latest turns)

in the last shadow of relief and redemption.

The urge to save myself leads me even to believe
there was an optical illusion: in the light you can see there
was nothing.

Even I want to escape and feel trapped,
I hear someone say: I remember that you …

I narrow my eyes to what I'm going to hear.
And go secretly, cloaking the present, name, profession.

But feel the flickering and clearly recognize
The blackest terror, breathing
love.

Spring 1988

The next poem is a text about writing, I think.

Consciousness –
first it produces the dead
then the living.

A death-eating plant,
so, that's how its life grows.

The death that it eats
must also grow:
until its full size

is *grown* into.

6/20/1994

I wrote the following poem during a poetry festival in the harbor town Rotterdam.

The feeling of profit
while thinking about poems as bearers of knowledge:

namely; what's-he-called is swimming up to the shoulders
and is surrounded by a general interest like a pond
as if it had in mind to explore what is
and definitely exists.

From this false height the eyes fall
on something at elbow height: business tips.

– Now, above it, wave green, water splashes on the quay.

11/18/1995

If I were to proceed from the form
then equally as from an existential one. That is, an equality
$$\text{of structures.}$$

Also searching while writing.
And searching while reading texts of others.

The second of which looks at the artwork's interests:
$$\text{how it succeeds.}$$
And: what does it bring?

What the first brings is success (or failure).
Success presupposes the conditions.

Beyond that, there is a poetological, innovative interest in writing and reading.
As if 1.) language were life (which it actually is);
    2.) the poem as individual were an independent subject.

At the same time, both are »on duty.«

When I find, read, the »one way or the other« there, I see that it can be better than the »one way or the other.« It results in this and this.

These are very general aspects that probably everyone
                                          knows:
views of the hereafter.

8/19/1998

Raw material, virgin

– a universal thinking that doesn't merely expose one's own part and/or attach itself to tradition acting as culture

thus also embracing
(each one's own)

no way, never:
The eye looking out for itself never has time to –
hunger (linger?). And begrudgingly.

This leads me (to now bring in what's below
the chin into play) – it leads me (assuming
I had asked) to consider the optical arrangement

as spontaneous, to expect, from the depths
of momentarily unused (while he sleeps) army boots,
pronouncements: ungrafted or: like truewood …

3/9/2000

Too bad that the particular impossibility isn't connected to its respective overcoming. They behave so senselessly towards one another. Senseless, as if little bits of what's dead were stuck everywhere between them. They're over us.

I am excited but also sad this morning. Color: green. The bit of what's dead: white or *even* worse. The don't-be-scared-color.

Just like it is impossible for me to imagine someone in Paris coming to the table, pulling out a chair and sitting. – No, go!

Between here and there and across the sea the world is coming to an end.

4/7/2000

An aesthetic impetus: I just thought that the aesthetic could have an existence that is so imposing, of a such a molding guiding force, that one would know and uphold the poetic speech and its forms, the realm of forms that probably arranges these forms with one another. A new tone, a new vibration that enters the body (something stationary like a standing army, which certainly has a function but doesn't function – unless it's in motion).

4/7/2000 on the same day

Does that which sets the tone constantly change?
How the ear measures today is questionable. Is a new tone added to a past construed as an eternal reservoir? One is not permitted to take anything without license, except in reviving, except with meaning …
There's a tension there but it probably listens with the big ear more than to the traditional piano.

4/12/2000

Poetry is vital for life. It performs social work and the only way it can do this is poetically.

4/12/2000 on the same day

– a new topic: the relationship of the other arts to poetry. It goes through *me* as a medium and continues to do its work with my means.
Just as I do it myself: making something a medium for its own sake, without asking.
Certainly that's not the case with the poetry that exists outside literature? Or is it? But of course: it doesn't even have to be written first!

4/13/2000

Why do I react differently when I come across literary failures of my own, any misplaced gesture or turn, differently perhaps than other officials on duty? Their space contains them, mine is open. That's what it needs. Absolutely, as one says, a free obligation.

A general terrain has been socially left. The ability to recognize is required. And provided. Liberating. Even when it cannot be taken up by others due to social constraints. Unless in liberating wrath.
Paul the Apostle was freed by a vision, that's how he became an apostle. Martyrdom was the consequence. Paul preached love as the free grace of God and test of faith.
Wrath.
One would have to call some of them victims, the others not, even though socially both are just as limited.
The question becomes passionate and hard when it asks about betrayal.
Betrayal is to make the claim that something else is impossible.
And that's just what upsets the likes of us, what keeps us alive.

6/29/2000

Poet, your public that's waiting for you is above all in your own soul!

7/6/2000

The I that rebels, that does not understand death, is probably the same one that, when it hears the words »adjacent room« (»it's in the adjacent room then«); reacts with irritation, as if to an imposition, after it had tolerated for awhile, not without nourishing itself from it, the sight of the river's width with the harbor warehouses on the other shore a couple of days before.

7/11/2000

The slight turns outward, those changes in someone, in someone's text, you can notice them, even if you didn't know the person before and do not always recognize the signs as concrete progress; they are transmitted due to a generalization-effect of the – in each case individual – general cage.

11/15/2000

I begin with lived existential situations, in the diary everything is aimed at them, views are taken and they develop during notation.
That's how they decide.

I know of no poetological pursuit without them.
– It doesn't interest me at first how a poem is to be built. Such that I would search for material for it. I don't go to given forms. Conversely: I write something and then look, oh, that's a sonnet. Once I even wrote a kind of sonnet, and once a haiku.

The haiku:

The poem appears.
As soon as it has appeared
It has disappeared.

12/9/2000 / 9/18/2016

Three-line poem

It's already getting dark in the heather.
Somehow you begin and end up with yourself.

Better than the other way around.

3/10/2001

One principle is for sure: a verse is a verse. If you mouth them without life then they slide together into one, like something screwed together on a bike. The undivided connection is like the unfixed, unarticulated.

on 9/23/2001

occurs to me that I never turn to my diary to write a poem.
There is no difference in the motive – which, by the way, is a nice word – between this and every other kind of excitation. Also a good word.
Only when setting the text in writing is a poetic structure indicated. More often, at the end, there is written »suspicion of a poem.« And often it can be recognized much later that there is indeed a structure. For example, in the most recent

books I have date stampings from previous years one after another, in the last book, »*Sonnenklar*« (»Crystal Clear«) they even go back to the previous century.

12/5/2001

Differences

Since the autumn, I have noticed that my diary entries, when they became poems, lacked a sense of harmony. These ones formed spaces, the others didn't.
An almost dislocatedly precise inward density in »Raw materials, virgin« in the book »*Sachverstand*« (»Expertise,« published in 2000).

I suppose that is one *type* of text.

The raw material type is passionate, extracts, intensifies, the other type demands servient discipline. Precision. Nothing flashes up there.

10/16/2004

It depends on me

That is a workpiece, waiting.
The workpiece in me is waiting.

Almost daily someone
or something comes, distracts.

Inside me, it is begging, angry.
Feels. Appeals. Workpieces.

No luring. Hardly any courage. I
am the fairy for it. If the fairy comes to it
it hopes, perks up. She gives it this and that
from her path. From which path?
The universal one.

From that one there, in the universal,
the universal path of things, the found
and the fallen, from the procedure that passes
over it, it receives this & that. It'd be good like that.

From that which just happens.
By chance. The workpiece then perks up.
It is a workpiece between death and life.
As between mountain and valley.

It is uncertain whether it stands a chance.

Remaining open, whether it stands a chance,
will count as one of its advantages
when it stands a chance.

As much in the whole as in the individual moves.

Waiting and staying open.
What belongs to it is a present participle principle.
                                        Progressive form.

Otherwise it won't work.
Then it might be good.
Then it is a fairy that comes like mercy.

But doesn't come when lured. Only as if it were ordered.
Indeterminate.
Comes uncertain. Pushes off. Trots like a dumb idiot
over to it, the one waiting.

It pokes. Begs.
It adds excruciating tension.

Removal is good.
It does me some good when I turn to it.
Although it does good, it doesn't lure me.

Its substances, matters
exist without me. Otherwise they wouldn't be its own!
It has to be that way.

»Without me« is a theme in this respect:
It separates, differentiates.

This is how indifference arises, I name it.
Indifference releases you and me.

To fail to be there
and to fail and to fail.

To be unfaithful. At the same time.
To pursue a subject, that doesn't belong to it, the workpiece.
And yet. In the background. In the failing.

The same formula applies, it rules, even otherwise:
I know I don't do what does me good.

A process from nothing else but me in which
it isn't me that decides, apparently.

Hopelessness dawns:
previous, numerous, even extinguished, perspectives.

Dawns like daylight,
so uncalled and unable to be led.

2/14/2007

»I owe nothing« – it harmonizes – after I presumably saw, seeingly presumed: I collect time in the same poem (and coronary vessel) that also absorbs the biological cultivation and induces spiritual maturity, this solving-it, dis-solve …

The word »speculate« knows this kind of perspective: a sensing, it seeks nothing, it finds, is called time, it is, to put it briefly: a transpiring. And of a positive nature, thanks to the pairing of the biological with the spiritual. I am hungry – I eat. You could also call such a succession a solution.
And conversely, a spiritual development could be called growth. Thus, it is certainly more than a mere finishing-off. The word poem is here meant to be the body's existence. And conversely the spiritual is meant to be the consummation. How it practices life in the poem is what gives the poem the dissolved individuality.

12/9/2007

Purification

Now the soul is unreachable

while its false reverberation
believes to signal exactly the opposite.

It is false but it believes nevertheless.

Look there, I say to myself,
into the black, the bottomless
absolute beyond.

You see the black there as fate, as straying
of the dependent, ill-fated
proprietress of a soul –

Everything could be everywhere here,
be justified

be here justified deceived,
just look, look on,

look behind – disappointed –
the sudden back flow of each and every
excitement.

N., as he was drunk so often,
and obtrusive
in the room

on this and that
white table.

Bleak. And behind it is – like clarity / purification –
then nothing but nothing,

nothing more than a drop in blood pressure
everywhere in your cells

under the usual tick marks
as if dead.

1/4/2008

Swing

It isolates itself defends itself
just wants to be there, it seems.

– ? No. Is enchained.
– Graying plumage nods downwards, sleeps.

One doesn't experience raised angel's wings.
Swinging like angels.

Only the harp-ell-wave, surging,
harp-playing-elbow-wave.

As while the cat is never the bird,
never: nonsense, a bird to no one,

but an ell elongated
ell without hand, to be fair,

but wave most likely in the tiger's
leap – tiger wave,

– and with less (the cat)
manages excellently

also is not ordinarily hunted,
grey cat of respectable, measured honor –

the grey cat and the orange, tabby, black –

Did you, like, plan to argue
that, damn it, devils are also winged –
at the beginning?

1/14/2008

It opens up: failure panorama landscape just as we can only grasp it in a single glance. A multiplicity, we see a landscape or something similar something static ... but it will be experienced in a complex dynamic whose movement »breaks down« the complexity in reading and experiencing.

As a result, there is no redemption as a fast apprehension. Rapid, unable to be stopped, at the same time complex, not simplifying.

(The prospect opens a failure)

What shows itself:
the edge collects all the ideas,
the middle is cloudy and sour.

That is in general: as if you were there and still there and will be there in the future.

Yesterday I was outside with music (too quiet), piano
– Schumann A number of small pieces. It was entertaining.
As soon as an increase in intensity surfaces, the amount of
effort in the labor on a text decays quickly –

What do you say to that –
The reflections here introduce a poem that captures, attests
to, extends the situation with its poetological bravura.

1/15/2008

The pleasure of inferring something from the ingredients, the pleasure of writing something, the trail from that to that. What I want to write, should have written

leads sharply outside, yes, hunts me, it lets me be sharply hunted, its object-subject, subject-object, which I am.

8/24/2009

– in fact, you could say that what had been overrun from outside is back in place and is looking, *yes*.

2/11/2012

Billionaires

Billion
numbers, mineral deposits
air
fertile soil
es

2/11/2012

Global level

Unimaginable poverty
and crime from poverty

The carriage chooses
the rig with the driver

6/12/2012, 6:47 AM

No

I don't want that one, I know that one, I don't want it.
I want a different one. One differently whisked.

Don't want to start the day from the one before.
Not dull continuation.

The peeping light
peeps from the balcony

tiles, falling plaster, chair frame.

»No connection.«

Alright fine, grandmother
I'll start the exercises immediately.

Awaken the muscle mass.
Fox, speak, how else.

1/11/2013

Weakness opinion speaks

I say / she says /
back & forth: I don't want
as if from some fundamental weakness
an opinion weakness speaks
a weakness opinion speaks

don't do enough for me
Unswervingly circumstances arise …

Find me vis-à-vis briefly
Don't give reasons

Vis-à-vis previously a tree
previously mountains
a lake
appear, persevere

Not I

Don't hold the scales
Wait, don't
give reasons

6/20/2014

That makes sense

The intelligent look (at something below – towards the text)
and the kind one – they are a carbon copy.
Makes sense!

10/14/2014

Origin of the poem: diary.

Heartache, lonely

Good advice is expensive there.

No one is there.

This nothing is inevitable.

10/18/2014

I was cold the whole day. Such a simple sentence. And I had always been considered incomprehensible. Well, not my fault. I'd bet such a sentence couldn't be found in any writing. – Hm, but probably something similar. No, but I mean *in writing*.

12/16/2014

Foreign country: Georgia.
The date of my trip cannot be determined exactly.
The first trip was with Adolf Endler and Rainer Kirsch in 1969 and then I went alone several times.

Memory abroad

From above it came,
from a clay yellow height,
the female rider (gypsy woman?)

colorfully dressed casual
sitting sideways
below

down on the clay yellow
path I was standing in front of a row
of three to five walnut trees
large, sturdy,

if I think about it,
it was definitely three to five

and not only just
three or four, it wouldn't have
been enough then for five,

which the female rider
would pass by later, before
she then rode by again
to the other side, abroad.

1/15/2015

In everything moving in parts, dividing further and coming together – visions and chocked fixed parts as well

One weeps for Mandelstam's wolfhound century as for the I of a goddess undivided severe Eruption Shattered anew and unending

Before that there was joy, as I walked outside, music in my stride and ear

2/7/2015

Pretty naïve:

11 PM – Just thought
– surrounded by totally dark night –

that it could also be pleasing
to pour the day down the drain

if you exert yourself.
Well – go ahead!

April 2015

The outs have (like
the sound says)

no garden.

7/9/2015

I'm reading in the bath: Nathalie Sarraute – »Fools Say«

»There is nothing more moving
in the world«*

mommommommo
The words themselves are moving.

* *Nathalie Sarraute, a French writer of Russian descent (born in 1900, died in Paris in 1999, according to Wikipedia »Fools Say« is a novel by her and the German translation is by Elmar Tophoven).*

August 2015

Maxim

Structural understanding: I have to interpret everything that comes from/to people as an outfit with a skeleton, just as the animal is pre-programmed and programmed as an entirety: we are much more pre-, but that is stuck, immobile enough, a living freshness, strength, is also held onto by a lack of knowledge about it etc.

8/9/2015

Wake up, sweating (look at the clock – 1:21 AM). Why doesn't the soul just let go of the anonymous burden or vice versa? It is also meish. A nice word. Every good mood is first earned, it seems, seems *to me*: where does it come from, the memory of *something*. Never *me*. Or procedure. Now the will was there again, the drive, this usual necessity (we are partners), to write down the takings, one of the industries of civilization, the me-part. Namely whereto in the computer. Is there anyone I can? The world werdly world of persons werd man, the person seems to know it.

Here in transcribing I come to several small surprises already, but not yet to the sense of them. They help to get on a wave of cheerfulness – fish jump, that is anonymous cheerfulness? almost. Writing it down, an escape came. The small black window – night next to me. And white within it, the open Trotsky books, after all, I'm now in bed without my glasses.

Go into the bathroom, keep reading, further and further into the Trotsky, slowly understanding, but now it pro-

ceeds steadily. For months. Good. Comprehending draws up passageways, perusals. Continue reading another piece with a pencil to underline, like yesterday, when it was no longer possible in the heat. Already 29 degrees. The good old big real summer that does its own thing, we are only qualities of it.
Well, in spite of the terribly traumatic – in the dream chamber – accounting, which is more often tormenting. This is the burden that even if you shirk it – »it isn't actually necessary, you don't need to do it right now« – dully claims its place.
While up here: I turn around, look to the other side, alongside it, the amazingly long brown roof beam. – Measure it: 3.17 meters long, my eyes thought: a tree so tall!

6:12. Woke up again, not happily, after around 3 hours sleep, uh-oh, the low blood pressure is back – had forgotten it. Rest awhile.

Not as violently.
8:30. Slept. But still the same: 27 degrees with an overcast sky.

9/17/2015

I don't want to say too much. I have a
well in my gourd. In the yard. Blackberries.
O. K.

3/10/2016 / 7/28/2017

Without a frame

Rural choral song
Tragedy = goat song – *tragos*: goat,
sings and dances with goat masks: choir.

From the sedentary, look!, outward.
Animal energy.

Otherwise yeah nothing but *this*
swing. In celebration.

Sing, sing, what happened …
No one was ever seen, right.
Five wild swans once migrated …

The legion knows it's one with the leader.

Oh, I'll flip a switch in my brain.
Around Arthur there was still no cult of the leader.
His knights rose from the lowest rank
into the noblest culture of nobility.

Did you ever want to have power? Right, never?

Who
wanted power. The
cretin Hitler, the underdeveloped
monster Stalin.

And what prescriptive pride
forced the upper classes to duel?

– Exactly *because* a subject leaves the context is why I follow it. Into that which opens up to it. That's when it lives.

3/19/2016

We were just talking (on the phone) and I don't know where it came from, the code word was »Alex.«

I was at the physical therapist and since the masseuse had loosened the muscles, I was still a little wobbly. As I came up to Alexanderplatz, two police officers stopped me, probably because of this, and demanded to see my ID. While they were looking at the ID, I asked, looking over them: »who are you looking for on this large empty square?«

Namely, while rabbits had erstwhile hopped on Alex in the discounted shrubbery, now one had to be proud of the two high-rises.

And Helga recounted that there was a Stasi car in front of her house and as she came out, she said: »I'm going now to the Alliance of Fine Artists, then to the supermarket and will be back in about an hour and a half.«

Today is 3/19/2016. I thought, I'll make a note of that.

A year later, I heard a further memory from Helga on the phone, for me it was a poem, it went like this:

The news

I – under the table – am 6.

When the war is over,
you'll be allowed to talk during meals.

Helga Paris, a friend of mine for a long time, is as old as me, and is a photographer and member of the Berlin Academy.

3/26/2016, 5:38 AM

Nothing more:

I am afraid in the void.
I am afraid to be afraid.

The pigeons coo, below is the earth,
ground. Black night. Oh, no,

I pulled up the roller blinds,
it's light already. –

10/3/2016

A reaction to Ernst Bloch: *Freiheit und Ordnung, Abriß der Sozialutopien* (Freedom and Order, Demolition of the Social Utopias), Reclam Leipzig 1985

The term class barriers – denotes an inhibition limiting the exploiting classes – the working class is not a class but rather the result of the exploiting class.
Ever since the »primitive society,« people have constantly built hierarchies.

The reason: by law there should be something right ...
The intellect takes a look there. Its meaning is: subsistence instead of extinction.
But ahead of it there is: Dingalingaling. Natural law is an invention of the intellect as a regime. Seventeenth century.

Reason can be blind, the intellect cannot.

The bureaucrat wants to be blind, otherwise he's gotta go,

for Jan Kuhlbrodt, my friend from Leipzig, he writes poems, novels and essays

12/14/2016

Suspicion of a poem

Lying on the bed, face down, reading

(recovering) (in spiritual discipline).

My lower back hurts a little.

As I become aware of it,

a bridge arch bulges high in front of me.

Why, I think, that now?

– I give my lower back air ...

Below we have a grass shore ... water ...

Suspicion of a poem.

5/29/2017

Diary pickings from the Bertelsmann Pocket Encyclopedia:

Pechenegs,

Tribal confederation of Turkic language family
Stem tree stem stemming from
stumpy

intermixed with Sarmantic and Finno-Ugric
groups

flew like seed clouds out of the air

»Ugric groups« Finno & Ugric mixed
when where how

semicolon

since the end of the ninth century
– after they were already out of this thus

… north of the Casp. sea, it says,
this unevenly cut light blue stocking,
on the earth, the largest inland lake

in conflict with the Khazars, it says,
of whom *were thrust direction W* (West), where

they **s**ettled
in **S**outh (*alliteration*)
Russia, lead **r**azzias (*further alliteration of* **r**)
in Byzantium, Hungary, **R**ussia
(*Russia is enormous*) till

*Yaroslav the Wise conquered
the* **P.** *in 1036.*

The lost **s** *of the alliteration above*. Forced back by the pursuing
Cumans into Hungary
and Bulgaria

(that's a fair bit but enough clowning about)

the **P.** sprouted roots
in the local

population.

Pechenegs.

It's the sibilant that does it.

I recognize this as a poem.

6/8/2017, 4 AM

Awake for about two hours now. Want to sleep. Turn the light off. Look to the right through the small window. Back there behind the foliage a red is crouching.

Read a magazine about Derrida, introduction p. 13: in the first phase (1962–72, born 1930) he was primarily »preoccupied« with the appearance or traces of »truth« and then the »focus was on aesthetic models and experiments« in the late 1970s. Thus, an increased aspiration regarding density.

– From there to the »Ethics of Discussion,« to a new theoretical approach.
Sentence:
»Lying awake next to the red sky of dawn.« – – –
Lights out. The white elderflowers are swaying in front of the window.
Lights on. I write it down. Maybe a text will come of it. If I could possibly be able to conjure up this Far Eastern subtlety (Japan, China).
(Not impossible.)

7/24/2017

Of course I am nervous while waiting for the Flixbus, I'm not driving it, I'm the object. For others, normal folks, this is not a problem, the object gains independence. For me, the writing subject, there's an objective inner subject conducting. They are something like partners. The inner seems to be deaf and blind. The outer is often surprised by the results.

8/5/2017

A strange observation in August: when I copy the diary entries I realize that I activate the language independently (beyond that which I commonly read), in fact in a natural, effortless way. Whether that is a developmental process? Since it is such a simple process, there would be hope that everyone could also do it. So that the common language would be mobilized. The standard efforts of poetic and scientific languages miss the mark on this process.

8/16/2017

Summer in the countryside

From time to time, here especially
I run out of the house

right around the house
to run as well

for some time

I'll stop here. The End.

12/31/2017

It occurs to me, dawns on my soul, that I have to do people some good at my readings, they should be aware of it. – If I want to, I also succeed.

– Last but not least another conclusion.

A poem is what it does.

I'll read one last poem from the book »*Sonanz*« (»Sonance«), of which one could say, the poem is what happens in it. Probably also a doing, and yet, one that is freer, from which the later ones have certainly profited. The time of its writing: 2002 to 2006.

7/8/2005

Warning

The world is full of fishhooks. Folk song and in chorus.
The world is full of folk songs. The valley is more empty
                                                                   deer antlers.
I dream creaks carts. Sunny morning, dream carts creak.

Behind the house the scenery a naked ribcage.
Breathing up and down. Ribs.

Kurzbiographien

Elke Erb, geboren 1938 in Scherbach/Eifel, 1949 Umzug der Familie nach Halle/DDR, Abitur, Studium der Pädagogik, Geschichte und Germanistik, Russisch an der Martin-Luther-Universität Halle/Saale. Ab 1963 Arbeit als Lektorin im Mitteldeutschen Verlag, danach freie Autorin, erste Veröffentlichungen ab 1968. Elke Erb schreibt Kurzprosa, Lyrik, prozessuale Texte, arbeitete als Herausgeberin und veröffentlichte zahlreiche Übersetzungen und Nachdichtungen, vor allem aus dem Russischen und aus dem Amerikanischen (Rosmarie Waldrop; mit Marianne Frisch).

Auszeichnungen: u. a. Peter-Huchel-Preis (1988), Heinrich-Mann-Preis (1990; zus. mit Adolf Endler), Erich-Fried-Preis (1995), Ida-Dehmel-Preis (1995), Norbert-C.-Kaser-Preis (1998), F.-C.-Weiskopf-Preis der Akademie der Künste Berlin (1999), Hans-Erich-Nossack-Preis für das Gesamtwerk (2007), Preis der Literaturhäuser (2011); Georg-Trakl-Preis (2012), Roswithapreis der Stadt Bad Gandersheim (2012), Erlanger Übersetzerpreis (2012), Ernst-Jandl-Preis für Lyrik (2013), Anke-Bennholdt-Thomsen-Lyrik-Preis der Deutschen Schillerstiftung 2015, Eduard-Mörike-Preis 2018.

Elke Erb, born in Scherbach/Eifel in 1938, moved with her family to Halle in the GDR in 1949, studied pedagogy, history, Russian and German Studies at the Martin Luther University of Halle/Saale. Began working as an editor at the Mitteldeutscher Verlag in 1963 then as a freelance author, first publications from 1968. Elke Erb writes short prose, poetry, procedural texts. She worked as an editor and published numerous translations and adaptations, especially from the Russian and American (Rosmarie Waldrop, with Marianne Frisch).

Awards: including, the Peter Huchel Prize (1988), Heinrich Mann Prize (1990; together with Adolf Endler), Erich Fried Prize (1995), Ida Dehmel Prize (1995), Norbert C. Kaser Prize (1998), F. C. Weiskopf Prize of the Berlin Academy of Arts (1999), Hans Erich Nossack Prize for her Œuvre (2007), Preis der Literaturhäuser (2011), Georg Trakl Prize (2012), Roswitha Prize of the City Bad Gandersheim (2012), the Erlangen Translation Prize (2012), Ernst Jandl Prize for Poetry (2013), the Anke Bennholdt-Thomsen Poetry Prize of the German Schiller Foundation (2015), Eduard Möricke Prize (2018).

Shane Anderson, geboren in San Jose, Kalifornien, Lyriker, Autor, Übersetzer. Er studierte Philosophie, und Komparatistik an der University of California, Davis. 2005 ging er nach Berlin, arbeitete als Übersetzer, Buchhändler und Autor. Sein erstes Buch »Études« erschien 2012; seine Übersetzung von Ulf Stolterfoths »Ammengespräche« (»The Amme Talks«) kam 2017 bei *Triple Canopy* heraus. Momentan arbeitet er an einem essayistischen Projekt »After the Oracle« über die Zusammenhänge von Basketball, Politik, Spiritualität und Ästhetik.

Born in San Jose, California, the poet, writer and translator Shane Anderson studied Philosophy and Comparative Literature at the University of California, Davis. Since moving to Berlin in 2005, he has worked as a translator, bookseller and writer. His first book, *Études*, was published in 2012 and in 2017 Anderson's translation of Ulf Stolterfoht's *The Amme Talks* was published by Triple Canopy. Currently, he is working on a creative nonfiction project, *After the Oracle*, about the intersections of basketball, politics, spirituality and aesthetics.